Radical Minds

Rethinking Theories of Intelligence

Freudian Trips

Copyright Page

Published by Omniterra Media Inc

First Edition

Visit the author's website at www.freudiantrips.com

Disclaimer

The views and opinions expressed in this book are those of the author(s) and do not necessarily reflect the official policy or position of any other agency, organization, employer, or company. The contents of this book are for informational and educational purposes only and are not intended to serve as professional advice, diagnosis, or treatment.

The information provided in this book is believed to be accurate and reliable as of the date of publication. However, it may include some errors or inaccuracies, and no warranty or guarantee is provided regarding the accuracy, timeliness, or applicability of the content.

Readers are encouraged to consult with professional philosophers, educators, or other qualified professionals where appropriate for personalized advice. The author(s) and publisher shall not be liable for any loss, damage, or harm caused or alleged to be caused, directly or indirectly, by the information or ideas contained, suggested, or referenced in this book.

By reading this book, the reader acknowledges and agrees that they are solely responsible for how they interpret and apply the information contained herein.

This book may also include references to other works, studies, and sources. These references are provided for further reading and exploration and do not imply endorsement or validation of the specific theories, viewpoints, or interpretations presented in those works.

Chapter 1: Mind Matters: An Intro to Intelligence

Welcome to the World of Intelligence!

Imagine this: you're at a party, and a magician pulls out a deck of cards. He asks you to pick a card, remember it, and put it back. Moments later, he reveals your chosen card, much to your astonishment! This magician, in many ways, represents the mystique and enigma of intelligence. Just like the card trick, understanding intelligence has been puzzling and fascinating humans for centuries.

A. What Exactly is Intelligence?

At its core, intelligence is our ability to think, learn, understand, and adapt. It's more than just getting top grades in school or being the quickest to solve a crossword puzzle. It's about how you approach a new situation, how you learn from your experiences, and how you use what you know to navigate the world around you.

Think about a toddler learning to walk. She stumbles, falls, yet she observes, adapts, and one day she's running around without a care!

This process - her ability to learn and adapt - showcases her intelligence.

B. Why Should We Care About Intelligence?

Imagine going through life without ever learning or adapting. You'd still be trying to eat with your hands instead of utensils, or trying to ride a bike without knowing how to balance. In essence, understanding intelligence helps us recognize why we can evolve, innovate, and create wonders like art, technology, and culture.

Plus, on a more personal level, appreciating the nuances of intelligence can also lead to greater empathy. We'll come to realize that being "smart" isn't one-size-fits-all. The artist who paints emotions, the mechanic who can 'listen' to a car's complaints, the dancer who speaks without words - all display intelligence in unique, beautiful ways.

C. A Sneak Peek into Our Journey

Now, you might be wondering, "Where is this book taking me?" Great question! Together, we're going on a journey through time and thought, delving into how our understanding of intelligence has evolved. From the classrooms with their IQ tests to the vibrant tapestry of global cultures with their unique interpretations, we're set for an exciting ride.

We'll encounter myths, challenge stereotypes, and even take a futuristic voyage into the realms of artificial intelligence. And in this adventure, we promise to keep things light, engaging, and free from confusing jargon. After all, the world of intelligence is for everyone to explore and understand!

Just like the magician at the party, the concept of intelligence has many tricks up its sleeve. As you flip through the pages of this book, get ready to be both the spectator and the participant, marveling at the revelations and discovering your own insights about the mind's magnificent capabilities.

Onward, fellow explorer! Let's unravel the mysteries of intelligence together.

Chapter 2: A Journey Through Time: How We've Understood Intelligence

The Grand Tapestry of Thought

Picture a vast landscape of ideas, stretching as far as the eye can see. This is the world of intelligence theories. It's grown and evolved over time, reflecting our changing understanding of the mind. Let's hop into our imaginary time machine and travel through some of the most significant moments in the history of intelligence theories!

A. The Birth of the IQ Test

Imagine you're in a classroom, pencil in hand, surrounded by rows of desks. Before you is a paper filled with questions, each one challenging you in a different way. This is the world of standardized testing—a realm where your intelligence is quantified with a number: the IQ (Intelligence Quotient).

In the early days, people believed intelligence could be neatly summed up with a single number. It was as if your brain was a muscle, and the IQ test was a way to measure its strength. These tests gained popularity as they were believed to predict a person's potential in academics and professions.

B. A Garden of Minds: The Gardner Theory

Now, shift your gaze from the classroom to a vibrant garden filled with diverse plants. Each plant represents a unique form of intelligence. This is the world seen through Howard Gardner's eyes.

Gardner didn't believe that intelligence was a one-size-fits-all concept. Instead, he proposed that we all possess multiple intelligences. Some of us are word-smart, while others excel in visual arts or musical talents. There are those who thrive in logical challenges, and some who are incredibly in tune with their bodies, like athletes or dancers.

In essence, Gardner's garden is a celebration of the diverse ways in which our minds bloom.

C. Feeling Smart: Goleman's World of Emotional Intelligence

Let's now float away from the garden and dive deep into a world filled with colors representing emotions. Welcome to the domain of Emotional Intelligence, an idea championed by Daniel Goleman.

You know those moments when you can 'read the room' or when you're incredibly in-tune with your own emotions? That's emotional intelligence in action. Goleman argued that our success in relationships, work, and even personal well-being isn't just based on how 'academically' smart we are. Instead, it's about understanding, managing, and using our emotions wisely.

D. A Thoughtful Pause: Reflecting on Our Journey

It's clear that our understanding of intelligence is as vast and varied as the world itself. From classrooms with their number scores to gardens filled with diverse talents and a world colored by emotions, the landscape of intelligence theories is a testament to the complexity of the human mind.

However, it's essential to remember that no single theory provides the entire picture. IQ tests have faced criticism for potentially oversimplifying intelligence and being influenced by factors like socio-economic conditions. Meanwhile, while Gardner's and Goleman's theories have been embraced for their holistic approach, they too face debates about their measurable aspects.

Our journey through time gives us a snapshot of the ever-evolving tapestry of intelligence theories. It reminds us that understanding the human mind is a continuous journey filled with discoveries, debates, and deeper insights.

As we continue our exploration in the chapters ahead, let's carry with us the wisdom from the past, celebrating the diversity of thought and the infinite ways in which our minds shine. Onward, explorer!

Chapter 3: Diving Deeper: The Bold Ideas of Intelligence

Journeying Beyond the Familiar

Imagine standing at the edge of a dense forest, eager to explore what lies beyond the familiar paths. This chapter is all about delving into the lesser-known, yet utterly fascinating, theories of intelligence that challenge the norm and stretch our imaginations.

A. The Success Factor: Sternberg's Model

Let's start with a question: What does it mean to be successful? For Robert Sternberg, success is all about adapting to, shaping, and selecting environments that fit your strengths. He coined this as the "Theory of Successful Intelligence."

It's like being a skilled chef. You need to know when to follow the recipe (analytical skills), when to improvise with ingredients (creative skills), and when to choose a particular cooking technique over another (practical skills). For Sternberg, intelligence is this mix of analytical, creative, and practical skills, working together to help us succeed in different situations.

B. The Three Musketeers of the Mind: The Triarchic Theory

This theory might sound similar to the one above, and that's because it is! Sternberg wasn't done with just one idea. His Triarchic Theory further breaks down intelligence into three main parts:

Analytical Intelligence: This is the problem-solving bit, like when you're trying to crack a tough puzzle.

Creative Intelligence: It's all about innovation. Think of moments when you come up with a brilliant new idea or solution.

Practical Intelligence: This is the street-smart aspect. It helps you navigate day-to-day tasks and understand what's needed in different situations.

Together, these three forms of intelligence work as a team, ensuring you're equipped for almost any challenge life throws your way.

C. Puzzle Pieces of the Brain: Modular Theories

Now, imagine your mind as a vast jigsaw puzzle, with each piece representing a specific skill or ability. Some pieces might be about language, others about memory or spatial awareness. Modular theories suggest that our intelligence is made up of these individual modules, each working independently.

It's like having specialized workers in a big factory. While one section handles packing, another deals with quality checks, and yet another with assembly. Each module (or section) has its unique task but contributes to the bigger picture.

D. Nature's Playground: The Bio-Ecological Theory

Have you ever noticed how plants in a garden respond differently depending on the sunlight, soil, and water they receive? The Bio-Ecological Theory applies a similar idea to intelligence. It suggests that our intelligence isn't just about what's in our genes, but also about the environment we grow up in.

Factors like culture, schooling, family, and even our friends play a significant role in shaping our intelligence. It's a dance between nature and nurture, where both partners are equally important.

E. Pausing for Thought: Evaluations and Discussions

Like every bold idea, these theories have sparked discussions and critiques. For instance:

While Sternberg's theories highlight a broader understanding of intelligence, some argue they're too expansive, making it challenging to measure or test these intelligences.

The modular approach, while fascinating, leads to questions about how these 'modules' communicate and integrate.

And the bio-ecological theory? It stirs debates about how much weight we should give to genetics versus environment.

But isn't that the beauty of exploration? Every theory, every idea, helps us inch closer to understanding the intricate tapestry of the human mind.

This chapter was all about exploring the unconventional, the theories that dare to think differently. As we journey further, let's celebrate the bold thinkers and their ideas, always remembering that intelligence is as vast and varied as the universe itself. Onward, explorer!

Chapter 4: Mapping Minds: The Crossroads of Brain Science and Measurements

Setting Sail on New Waters

Let's imagine intelligence as a vast ocean. While we've previously looked at the different islands (theories) in this ocean, now we'll dive beneath the surface, exploring the deep interplay between our brain's workings and the tools we use to measure intelligence.

A. The Marvel of the Brain: Unraveling Neurological Connections

Imagine the most intricate spider web, shimmering in the morning dew. That's somewhat like our brain—a sprawling network of connections, with each thread representing a neural pathway. These pathways light up like twinkling stars when we think, solve problems, or get creative.

Some regions of our brain get particularly active when we engage in tasks that test our intelligence. For example:

The frontal lobe, right behind your forehead, helps with problem-solving and decision-making.

The parietal lobe, sitting at the top and back of your head, assists in processing information, including mathematical tasks.

Essentially, when we talk about intelligence and the brain, we're trying to figure out which parts of our "web" glow brightest when we're at our cognitive best.

B. Measuring the Mind: The World of Psychometrics

Have you ever wondered how tests, like those IQ ones we talked about earlier, are created? Enter the realm of psychometrics—the science of measuring our mental abilities.

It's like building a ruler for the mind. Psychometricians (the scientists who specialize in this) create tests ensuring they are reliable (you'd get similar scores if you took the test multiple times) and valid (the test truly measures what it claims to).

In essence, psychometrics tries to turn abstract concepts, like intelligence, into something tangible and measurable.

C. Walking a Tightrope: The Tricky Side of Intelligence Research

Like any exploration, venturing into the brain's depths and trying to measure its capabilities isn't without challenges.

Limitations: No test is perfect. For instance, while an IQ test might measure certain cognitive abilities, it might not capture creativity or emotional understanding.

Ethical Considerations: Intelligence research can sometimes lead to labeling or stereotyping. Remember the danger of saying one group is "smarter" than another based on skewed or biased testing? That's a big no-no.

It's crucial to approach this research with an open mind and a responsible heart, ensuring that we don't misuse or misinterpret the findings.

D. Reflections and Ruminations

While the intersection of neuroscience and psychometrics offers thrilling insights, it's vital to tread with caution. Critics often point out:

The brain is more complex than we currently understand. Pinning intelligence to specific areas might be oversimplifying things.

Psychometric tests, while useful, are just tools. They can't define or limit a person's potential. After all, we're all more than just a score, right?

By grappling with these critiques, we ensure that our journey into understanding intelligence is both rigorous and compassionate.

This chapter took us on a whirlwind tour from the intricacies of our brain to the tools we've crafted to measure its prowess. It's a testament to humanity's relentless curiosity and the quest to understand the most profound of its mysteries—ourselves.

Stay curious, dear reader. The adventure continues!

Chapter 5: Minds of Metal: The World of Artificial Intelligence and Us

A New Frontier in Understanding

Imagine a bustling city in a science fiction tale. Skyscrapers gleam, hovercars zip by, and among the crowds, you spot robots interacting seamlessly with humans. This vision isn't too far off from our present. As we advance in technology, especially in the realm of Artificial Intelligence (AI), we're prompted to ponder: How does machine intelligence compare to ours?

A. When Silicon Meets Neurons: The Dance of AI and Human Intelligence

Think of the most complicated jigsaw puzzle you've ever seen. Human intelligence is like that – multifaceted and nuanced. We think, feel, dream, create, and so much more. Now, imagine a highly efficient computer program adept at solving this puzzle. That's AI for you.

Similarities: Both human brains and AI can process information, learn from experiences (though in different ways), and solve problems.

Differences: While we're driven by emotions, beliefs, and consciousness, AI operates on data and algorithms. It doesn't "feel" joy or sadness, nor does it dream or ponder life's mysteries.

B. Passing the Turing Test: The Measure of Machine Minds

Picture a game show. On one side, there's a robot, and on the other, a human. Behind a curtain, there's a judge, communicating with both. If the judge can't reliably tell who's the robot and who's the human based on their answers, the robot is said to have passed the "Turing Test," a concept introduced by Alan Turing, a pioneering computer scientist.

This test was one of the first attempts to measure machine intelligence. But as AI has grown more sophisticated, many believe we need even more nuanced tests to truly gauge a machine's cognitive prowess.

C. AI's Influence on Our Understanding of Ourselves

It's intriguing how AI, a product of human ingenuity, pushes us to reflect deeper on our own intelligence.

Rethinking Capacities: As machines excel in tasks once thought exclusive to humans (like playing chess or creating art), we're prompted to ask: What truly sets us apart?

New Research Avenues: AI models, inspired by our neural networks, have given scientists fresh insights into how our brains might function. On the flip side, understanding our intelligence has inspired more advanced and nuanced AI designs.

D. A Mirror of Critiques and Reflections

Our journey into the realm of AI is not without its challenges and critiques:

The Limits of AI: While machines can mimic certain aspects of human intelligence, they lack consciousness, emotions, and the richness of human experiences.

Ethical Concerns: There are valid fears about AI surpassing human intelligence, potential job losses, and the misuse of AI in areas like surveillance.

Redefining Intelligence: Some argue that comparing AI and human intelligence is like comparing apples and oranges. They're inherently different and maybe shouldn't be measured on the same scale.

Beyond the Horizon: A World with AI

As we wrap up this chapter, consider this: the very existence of AI, machines designed to think and learn, is a testament to the marvel of human intelligence. As we stride forward into a world where silicon minds coexist with organic ones, let's embrace the opportunity to understand, innovate, and co-create a harmonious future.

Remember, the true magic lies not just in understanding but in the wondrous journey of discovery. Forward, explorer, to uncharted territories!

Chapter 6: Through Many Lenses: Intelligence in the Tapestry of Cultures

An Invitation to a Global Feast

Imagine attending a global banquet, where every dish, every flavor is unique, representing the rich diversity of our world. Our understanding of intelligence is somewhat like this feast. Each culture, each society offers its own definition and value to what it means to be 'intelligent'. Come, let's indulge in this array of perspectives.

A. Crafting Intelligence: The Role of Societal Views

Imagine growing up in a world where the ability to tell gripping stories is the highest form of intelligence. In another place, perhaps it's the skill of navigating the sea by reading the stars.

Society often acts as a mirror, reflecting what it values most. Over time, these values can shape how intelligence is perceived:

Bias and Influence: From the books we read to the movies we watch, our idea of 'smart' or 'intelligent' is often influenced by societal biases. For example, why is a math whiz often portrayed as more intelligent than a skilled dancer?

Shifting Sands: What's considered intelligent today might not have been the same a century ago, or even a decade ago. As societies evolve, so do their definitions.

B. A World of Wisdom: Intelligence across the Globe

Each corner of our vast world has its own unique lens to view intelligence:

Eastern Perspectives: In many Asian cultures, intelligence isn't just about individual prowess but also about understanding one's place in the larger community and harmoniously blending in.

African Views: Many African societies value practical skills, storytelling, and community leadership as markers of intelligence.

Western Thoughts: There's often an emphasis on individual achievement, innovation, and analytical abilities.

Remember, no perspective is 'right' or 'wrong'. They're just different, like the diverse dishes at our global banquet.

C. The Web of Society: Systems, Structures, and Intelligence

Think of a vast spiderweb, with each thread interwoven tightly. Our society's structures—like education, media, and even politics—play crucial roles in shaping our understanding of intelligence:

Education's Role: Schools often reward certain types of intelligence (like memorization or analytical thinking) while sidelining others (like creativity or emotional understanding).

The Media Effect: From showcasing genius detectives in TV shows to reporting on child prodigies, media can influence what we see as 'intelligent'.

Power Play: Historically, those in power sometimes defined intelligence to maintain status quo, often leading to biases against certain groups or cultures.

D. Pausing for Reflection: Questions and Conversations

Like any complex tapestry, the sociocultural perspectives on intelligence invite both admiration and critique:

Blind Spots: Are we missing out on recognizing diverse forms of intelligence because of our biases?

Universal vs. Local: Is there a universal definition of intelligence, or should it always be context-specific?

Evolving Ideas: As our world becomes more interconnected, how might our understanding of intelligence change?

The Dance of Cultures: A Closing Thought

As we wrap up our journey across continents and cultures, let's celebrate the richness of perspectives. Let's embrace the idea that intelligence is multifaceted, ever-evolving, and beautifully diverse. After all, it's this diversity that adds color, depth, and vibrancy to the human tapestry.

Cheers to the endless wonder of learning, growing, and understanding! Onward to new horizons!

Chapter 7: Tomorrow's Mindscape: Charting the Unknown Realms of Intelligence

Gazing into the Crystal Ball

Have you ever sat under a starry sky, looking up, and wondering about the infinite possibilities of the universe? The future of intelligence feels a lot like that—a realm filled with questions, speculations, and awe-inspiring potential. Buckle up; we're setting sail into the uncharted territories of tomorrow's intelligence!

A. Decoding the Blueprint: Genetics and Biotech's Promise

Picture a vast library, every book brimming with stories, secrets, and instructions. That's a bit like our DNA—nature's blueprint. With advancements in genetics and biotechnology, we're beginning to read and, sometimes, even edit these stories.

Boosting Brainpower? Imagine if, in the future, tweaks to our DNA could enhance our cognitive abilities or memory. Sounds like a sci-fi tale, right? But with the rise of CRISPR and other biotechnologies, it's a future that's not too far off.

Ethical Echoes: While promising, such advancements beckon profound questions. Should we edit genes for intelligence? Where do we draw the line?

B. The Quantum Quandary: Merging Mind and Physics

You've probably heard of quantum physics—nature's rulebook for the smallest particles. Now, imagine if this tiny realm held secrets to understanding our intelligence.

The Quantum Brain: Some scientists speculate that our brain might operate on quantum principles, making our thinking process incredibly fast and efficient.

From Fiction to Fact: While the idea sounds straight out of a futuristic novel, ongoing research hints that this theory might have legs to stand on. Who knows? Tomorrow's intelligence might be a blend of biology and quantum wonders.

C. The Great Dance: Intelligence Meets Consciousness

What makes us, well, us? Is it our intelligence—the way we think, learn, and solve problems? Or is it our consciousness—the deep sense of awareness, the 'I' that experiences emotions, dreams, and thoughts?

Twins or Strangers? As we advance, the line between intelligence and consciousness might blur. Could AI ever become conscious? Can consciousness be enhanced alongside intelligence?

The Ultimate Quest: Understanding the dance between intelligence and consciousness might just be humanity's most profound journey, a path to unlocking our fullest potential.

D. Reflections from Tomorrow: Praises and Pitfalls

As with any venture into the unknown, our speculations about the future of intelligence invite both excitement and critique:

The Wonder: Advancements in genetics, quantum theory, and consciousness research promise a future where we might understand and tap into our intelligence like never before.

The Warnings: With great power comes great responsibility. Ethical dilemmas, potential misuses, and even philosophical debates about the nature of intelligence await us.

Embracing Humility: It's vital to approach these frontiers with both curiosity and caution, cherishing the mysteries as much as the answers.

To the Horizon and Beyond

As our chapter concludes, let's bask in the wonder of possibilities. The future of intelligence might be filled with questions, but isn't that what makes the journey thrilling? As we stand at the crossroads of today and tomorrow, let's dream, ponder, and stride forth with hope and imagination.

For in seeking, we grow; in wondering, we discover. To the future, dear reader, with stars in our eyes and dreams in our hearts!

Chapter 8: Coming Full Circle: Where We've Been and Where We Might Go

A Journey Revisited

Just as a river flows, winding its way through diverse terrains, our exploration of intelligence has meandered through history, science, culture, technology, and speculation. As we near the river's mouth, let's pause to reflect on the vibrant tapestry of ideas we've woven together.

A. The Mosaic of Intelligence: Recollecting Our Journey

The Foundations: We began by examining age-old perceptions of intelligence, where IQ tests and standardized measurements took center stage.

Diverse Lenses: We then donned different glasses, peering at Howard Gardner's multiple intelligences, diving into the depths of emotional intelligence, and soaring with the radical and controversial theories.

The Brain and Beyond: A stopover at the neuroscience station helped us understand the intricate dance of neurons and thoughts. We also probed into the meticulous methods of psychometrics.

Machines and Minds: The realm of artificial intelligence posed thought-provoking questions about the nature of cognition itself.

A Cultural Sojourn: We ventured into the vast landscapes of societal and cultural interpretations, realizing intelligence is as varied as the myriad cultures that dot our globe.

Gazing Forward: With an imaginative leap, we delved into future speculations, grappling with quantum quandaries, genetic promises, and the enigmatic dance of consciousness.

B. The Horizon Beckons: What Lies Ahead?

A Genetic Revolution: With biotechnologies advancing at breakneck speed, might we see a day where our DNA holds the key to enhanced cognitive abilities?

The Quantum Conundrum: Will future researchers crack the code, revealing if our brain indeed operates on quantum principles?

Conscious Choices: As AI progresses, ethical decisions about machine intelligence, consciousness, and their implications will be paramount.

Global Intelligence: As the world becomes more interconnected, collaborative research spanning cultures, disciplines, and methodologies could redefine our understanding of intelligence.

C. An Invitation to Wonder, Question, and Engage

Dear reader, while this book has aimed to elucidate the complexities of intelligence, the true journey starts now, with you. Embrace these ideas, not as definitive answers, but as starting points for your own exploration.

Stay Curious: Delve deeper into topics that piqued your interest. Remember, every expert was once a beginner, fueled by curiosity.

Challenge the Status Quo: Just as theories have evolved, your questions and critical thinking might pave the way for newer perspectives.

Engage in Dialogue: Share these ideas with friends, family, or even strangers. Through discussions, we often gain fresh insights and broaden our horizons.

Embarking on New Adventures

As we close this chapter and the book, envision yourself at the edge of a vast ocean, the waters representing the infinite mysteries of intelligence. Though our journey together concludes here, countless adventures await you.

Dive in, explore, question, and cherish the wonders of the human mind. For in the realm of intelligence, the journey itself is the reward. Wishing you a voyage filled with discoveries and joys!

About Freudian Trips

Welcome to Freudian Trips, your dedicated platform for diving deep into the world of psychology. We are more than just a YouTube channel or a book publisher. We are a beacon of enlightenment, making complex psychological concepts accessible and engaging for all.

Our YouTube channel is a rich repository of psychology made simple. We take the profound and often complex ideas from the world of psychology and break them down into digestible, easy-to-understand content. From the foundational theories of Freud to the cognitive insights of Piaget, we cover a broad spectrum of psychological schools and thoughts, making psychology accessible to everyone, regardless of their background or prior knowledge.

As a book publisher, we take the same approach, transforming intricate psychological theories into comprehensible narratives. Our books are not just collections of words, but vessels of wisdom that make psychology approachable and relatable. We believe that psychology should not be confined to academic circles, but should be available to all who seek to understand the human mind and behavior.

At Freudian Trips, we believe in the power of curiosity and the pursuit of knowledge. We are here to stoke the fires of your curiosity, to guide you on your intellectual journey, and to help you navigate the fascinating world of psychology.

If you are someone who is not afraid to question, to explore, and to learn, then you are in the right place. Join us on this journey of exploration, as we make psychology easy to understand, one concept at a time.

Be sure to visit our Youtube channel at: www.freudiantrips.com/youtube

You can also visit us on the web at www.freudiantrips.com

Welcome to The Freudian Trip community. Stay curious. Stay enlightened.